LeBron James

ABDO
Publishing Company

A Big Buddy Book
by **Sarah Tieck**

VISIT US AT
www.abdopublishing.com

Published by ABDO Publishing Company, 8000 West 78th Street, Edina, Minnesota 55439.

Printed in the United States.

Coordinating Series Editor: Rochelle Baltzer
Contributing Editors: Heidi M.D. Elston, BreAnn Rumsch, Marcia Zappa
Graphic Design: Maria Hosley
Cover Photograph: *AP Photo*: Paul Battaglia
Interior Photographs/Illustrations: *AP Photo*: Alex Brandon (p. 20), Chuck Burton (pp. 7, 10), Mark Duncan (pp. 9, 11, 13, 15, 16), Eric Gay (p. 19), Darren Hauck (p. 16), Bill Kostroun (p. 23), Hector Mata (p. 5), Dale Omori/ The Plain Dealer (p. 8), Stuart Ramson (p. 15), Amy Sancetta (p. 28), Sipa via AP Images (p. 25), Matt Slocum (p. 29), Pat Sullivan (p. 20), Dusan Vranic (p. 25), Steve C. Wilson (p. 23); *Getty Images*: © 2009 NBAE/Andrew D. Bernstein/NBAE via Getty Images (p. 27).

Library of Congress Cataloging-in-Publication Data

Tieck, Sarah, 1976-
  LeBron James : basketball superstar / Sarah Tieck.
    p. cm. -- (Big buddy biographies)
  ISBN 978-1-60453-708-6
  1. James, LeBron--Juvenile literature. 2. Basketball players--United States--Biography--Juvenile literature. I. Title.

GV884.J36T54 2009
796.323092--dc22
ʹ[B]
                                         2009011717

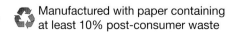

LeBron
James

Contents

Basketball Star

LeBron James is a famous and talented basketball player. He is known for joining the Cleveland Cavaliers at a young age.

Some people say LeBron is one of the best National Basketball Association (NBA) players ever! He has set many records.

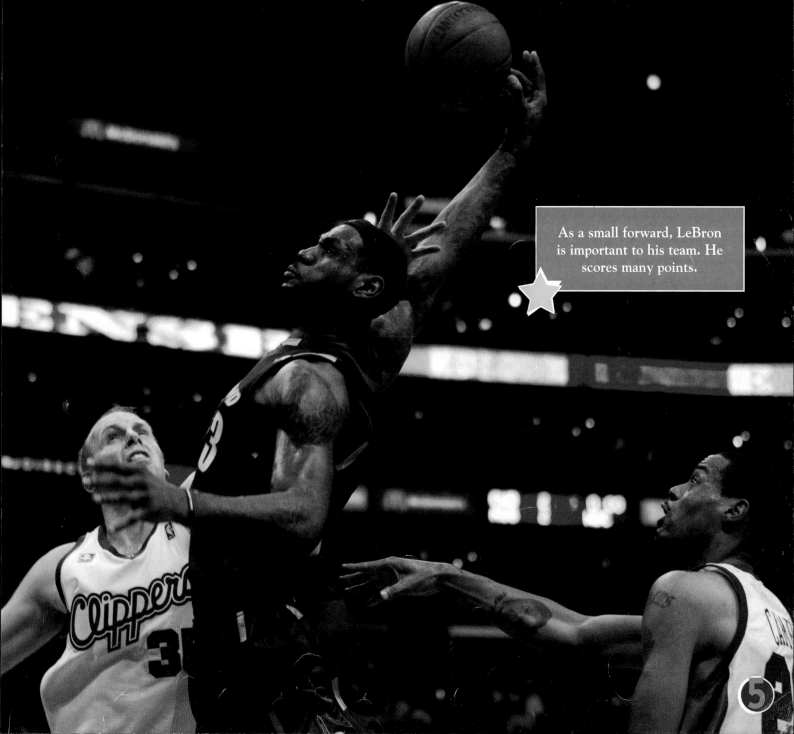

As a small forward, LeBron is important to his team. He scores many points.

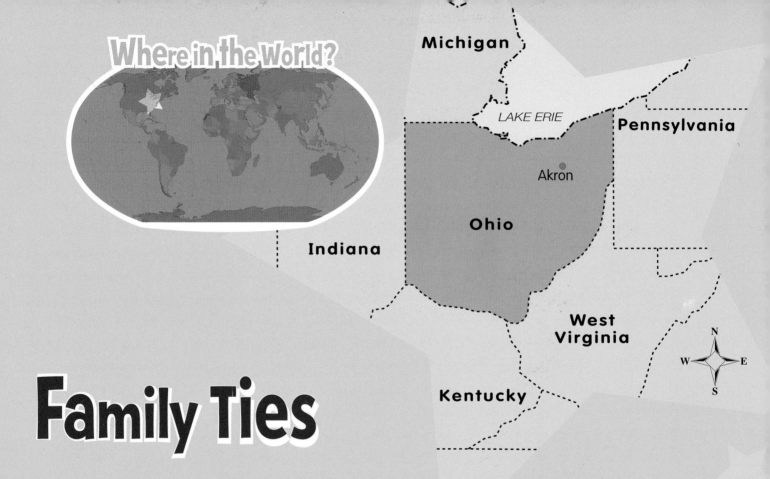

Michigan

LAKE ERIE

Pennsylvania

Akron

Ohio

Indiana

West Virginia

Kentucky

N
W   E
S

Family Ties

LeBron Raymone James was born in Akron, Ohio, on December 30, 1984. His parents are Gloria James and Anthony McClelland. LeBron has no brothers or sisters.

LeBron's mother was young when he was born. His father was not part of his life. Gloria's family helped her raise LeBron.

Gloria often attended LeBron's high school basketball games. Some say she is still LeBron's biggest fan.

Did you know...

Sometimes Gloria calls LeBron "Bron Bron."

7

Growing Up

As a young boy, LeBron enjoyed sports. Around age eight, he started playing football and basketball. One of his **coaches**, Frankie Walker, recognized LeBron's talent. He also noticed that LeBron missed a lot of school.

Frankie soon learned Gloria was having trouble caring for LeBron. So, he invited LeBron to live with his family. The Walkers made sure LeBron went to school. They treated him like family.

By eighth grade, LeBron was more than six feet (2 m) tall! In high school, LeBron (*center*) towered over many of his teammates.

After living with the Walkers, LeBron
stayed close with the family. He sometimes
joined them for birthdays and holidays.

In high school, LeBron was close friends with his teammates. He was part of a group that called itself the "Fab Four."

People were very excited about LeBron's talent. Fans called him "King James." They believed he would become an NBA player.

School Years

LeBron attended Saint Vincent-Saint Mary High School in Akron. He played football and basketball there. Soon, it became clear that LeBron was a basketball star. He helped his team win many games, including state **competitions**!

By his third year, LeBron was becoming famous for his basketball skills. People traveled from all over to watch LeBron play. Even famous basketball players, such as Shaquille O'Neal, were filling the seats.

LeBron's school gym became too small for all his fans. So, some games were moved to the University of Akron.

Did you know...

Basketball star Michael Jordan is one of LeBron's heroes. When LeBron was just 16, Michael noticed him. He even invited LeBron to work out with him and some other NBA players!

Some of LeBron's high school basketball games were shown on national television! LeBron also appeared in magazines and newspapers.

Going Pro

After high school, LeBron wanted to play **professional** basketball. During the 2003 NBA **draft**, LeBron was the first player chosen for a team! The Cleveland Cavaliers picked him. He became their newest small forward.

LeBron proved to be a **valuable** team member. During his first season, LeBron became the youngest NBA player to score more than 40 points in a game!

Did you know...

Small forwards play in the middle of the action. Even though their main goal is scoring points, small forwards are often considered all-purpose players. They help set up plays for their team.

Cleveland Cavaliers manager Jim Paxson (*left*) was excited when LeBron joined his team in 2003. The next year, LeBron (*right*) was named Rookie of the Year for his accomplishments!

LeBron has size 16 feet! Shoe companies create shoes just for him! Sometimes, the shoes are given to fans.

Did you know...

In 2005, LeBron broke another record. He became the youngest NBA player to score more than 50 points in one game!

LeBron is considered one of the most talented basketball players. He has achieved many things as a young player.

During the 2004–2005 season, LeBron continued to advance his skills. That season, he scored the most field goals of any NBA player. And, he had the most minutes of playing time in the league.

The Cavaliers played the San Antonio Spurs in the 2007 NBA Finals. The Spurs won in four games.

Rising Star

LeBron has proven himself an important part of the Cleveland Cavaliers. He has helped his team win many games. Their overall number of wins has improved!

The Cavaliers made the NBA **play-offs** in 2006, 2007, 2008, and 2009. In 2007, they beat the Detroit Pistons. This meant they had won the NBA Eastern Conference Finals. So, the Cavaliers went on to the NBA Finals for the first time ever!

The NBA All-Star MVP receives a special trophy.

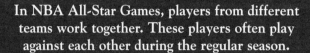

In NBA All-Star Games, players from different teams work together. These players often play against each other during the regular season.

LeBron has been recognized for his great skill on the court. Each year from 2005 to 2009, he was named an NBA All-Star. Fans and NBA **coaches** choose All-Star players.

As an All-Star, LeBron played in the yearly All-Star Game. In this **competition**, the Eastern Conference All-Stars play against the Western Conference All-Stars. LeBron was named the Most **Valuable** Player (MVP) for this game in 2006 and 2008.

Awesome Talent

LeBron has set many NBA records as a young player. Many people compare him to basketball star Michael Jordan.

Michael is often considered the greatest basketball player of all time. Already, LeBron is having similar success to Michael. And, LeBron is still improving!

LeBron (*left*) used to wish he'd grow as tall as Michael Jordan (*right*). Now, LeBron is about six feet eight inches (2 m) tall. This makes LeBron about two inches (5 cm) taller than Michael!

Olympic Champion

LeBron is a member of the U.S. Olympic basketball team. He played basketball with Team USA in the 2004 and 2008 Olympic Summer Games.

It is an honor to take part in the Olympics. Athletes from around the world **compete** to win Olympic medals.

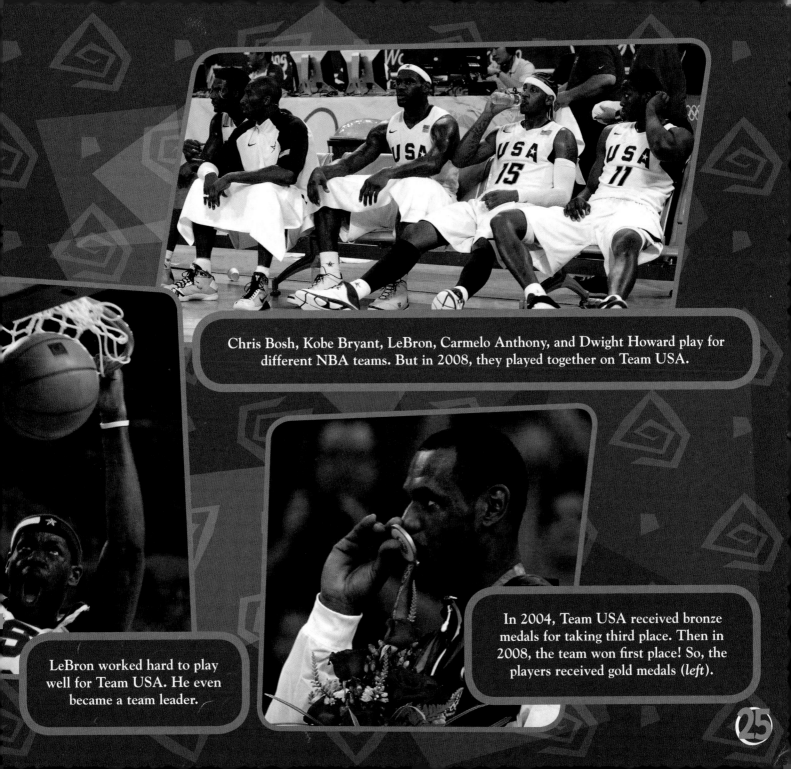

Chris Bosh, Kobe Bryant, LeBron, Carmelo Anthony, and Dwight Howard play for different NBA teams. But in 2008, they played together on Team USA.

LeBron worked hard to play well for Team USA. He even became a team leader.

In 2004, Team USA received bronze medals for taking third place. Then in 2008, the team won first place! So, the players received gold medals (*left*).

25

Off the Court

LeBron is known worldwide for his basketball skills. He is often featured in magazines and newspapers.

LeBron spends his free time with his family. He has two sons. LeBron James Jr. was born on October 6, 2004. And, Bryce Maximus James was born on June 14, 2007.

Did you know...

LeBron likes to help others. In 2004, he and his mother started the LeBron James Family Foundation. It helps children in need.

Being a good father to Bryce (*left*) and LeBron Jr. (*right*) is important to LeBron.

LeBron received his MVP award at Saint Vincent-Saint Mary High School.

Buzz

During the 2008–2009 season, LeBron improved his game. He even won his first NBA MVP award! Also in 2009, the Cavaliers made the NBA play-offs. However, they lost in the Eastern Conference Finals.

Fans expect great things from LeBron James. Many believe he has a bright future. They look forward to his continued success.

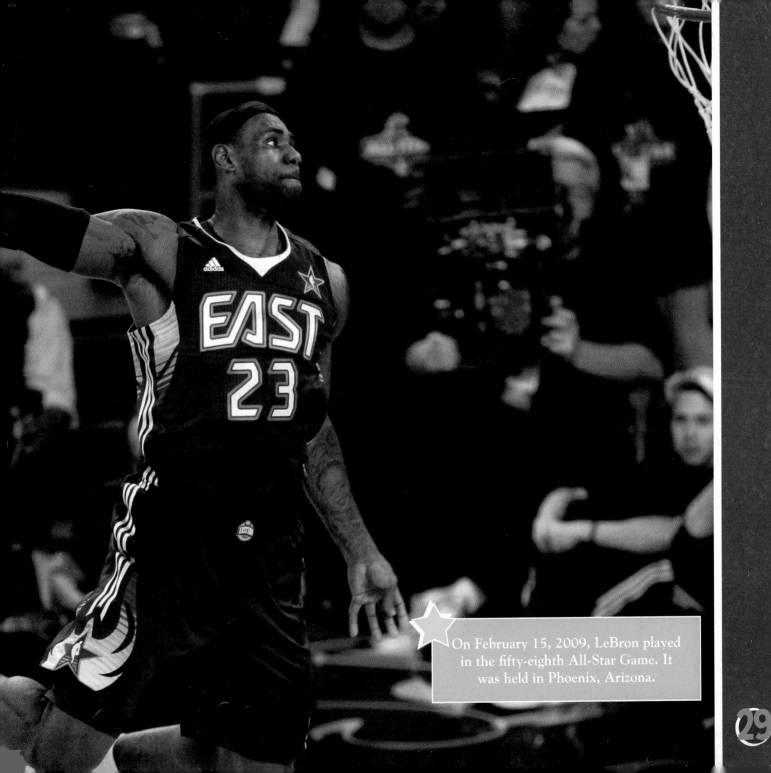

On February 15, 2009, LeBron played in the fifty-eighth All-Star Game. It was held in Phoenix, Arizona.

Snapshot

★**Name**: LeBron Raymone James

★**Birthday**: December 30, 1984

★**Birthplace**: Akron, Ohio

★**Turned professional**: 2003

★**Plays with**: Cleveland Cavaliers

★**Position**: Small forward

★**Number**: 23

Important Words

coach someone who teaches or trains a person or a group on a certain subject or skill.

competition (kahm-puh-TIH-shuhn) a contest between two or more persons or groups. To compete is to take part in a competition.

draft an event during which sports teams choose new players.

field goal any basket scored, other than a free throw. A field goal is worth either two or three points.

future (FYOO-chuhr) a time that has not yet occurred.

play-off a series of games leading to a final match to find a winner.

professional (pruh-FEHSH-nuhl) working for money rather than for pleasure.

valuable of great use or service.

Web Sites

To learn more about LeBron James, visit ABDO Publishing Company online. Web sites about LeBron James are featured on our Book Links page. These links are routinely monitored and updated to provide the most current information available.

www.abdopublishing.com

Index